Where The Bears Are
A Kid's Guide to Yosemite National Park, USA

Photography By John D. Weigand
Poetry By Penelope Dyan

Bellissima Publishing, LLC
Jamul, California
www.bellissimapublishing.com

copyright © 2011 by Penny D. Weigand and John D. Weigand

All rights reserved. No part of this book may be
reproduced or transmitted in any form or by any means,
electronic or mechanical, including photocopying,
recording, or by any other means, or by any information or
storage retrieval system, without permission from the publisher.

ISBN 978-1-61477-019-0
First Edition

The richness I achieve comes from Nature, the source of my inspiration.

-Claude Monet-

Introduction

Right there in California, just up the coast from Disneyland and Hollywood, past Bakersfield and Fresno, past a few small towns is where you will find Yosemite National Park, one of the very first wilderness parks of the United States. Yosemite is best known for its waterfalls, but within its nearly 1,200 square miles, you will also find deep valleys, meadows, ancient giant sequoias, and more. Concerned citizen Galen Clark and others, and Senator John Conness advocated for protection of Yosemite from commercial interests. A park bill was prepared with the assistance of the General Land Office in the Interior Department. The bill passed both houses of the 38th United States Congress, and was signed by President Abraham Lincoln on June 30, 1864, creating the Yosemite Grant, the first instance of park land being set aside for preservation and public use by the U.S. federal government. (Next came the 1872 creation of Yellowstone National Park.)

Award winning author, attorney and former teacher, Penelope Dyan and photographer, John D. Weigand have combined efforts to show you some of the Yosemite Valley, but just those things a kid would really like to see. Look through a child's eyes, let your child make this book his or her own and add photos, postcards, notes and drawings to it, and explore Yosemite and be inspired!

Where The Bears Are
A Kid's Guide to Yosemite National Park, USA

Photography By John D. Weigand
Poetry By Penelope Dyan

In the Yosemite Valley there is
a lodge where you can stay.
Everything is close
and not too far away.
You can take the shuttle bus;
or if you want, you could hike.
Or if you are so inclined,
you could even ride a bike!

And practically right outside
your own hotel door,
you can see the Yosemite Falls
and so much more!

There is a beautiful mountain that reaches up to the sky. I think they call it the Sentinel, but I really don't know why.

In the Yosemite Museum
an Indian points the way,
right to a little piece
of what was yesterday.

You can see Indian teepees
(houses made all of wood)
and how Indians took
and used nature
for the common good.

This was the chief's house (much bigger than the rest) where the chief of the tribe could invite a special guest.

The ceremonial house
is still used today,
in exactly the same ritual way.
There is a sign that tells you:
KEEP OUT!
You cannot go inside
and simply run about.

This is where black acorns
were stored
(the main food the Indians ate)
they ground the acorns
so they could make
delicious bread and other things
for their dinner plates.

Along this bridge you can go;
but it is not meant for running,
so please walk slow!
No one wants you to slip or fall.
For that would be a tragedy,
after all. . .

If into the Merced River
you took a big tumble,
Your mother would do SO much
more than JUST grumble!
And the water in the river
is oh so VERY cold,
and full of slimy fish and things,
so your mother's hand
PLEASE HOLD!

You can peek through a tree.
Walk through it if you're three!
Keep your eyes open wide; but
from your mother do NOT hide.
You can see so much
when you are a child,
in Yosemite Park,
out there in the wild.
BUT if way far in the distance
you HAPPEN to see a bear
ever so quietly,
get right OUT of there!

And then you can visit again
this Indian's house,
maybe see a dear, a squirrel,
a bird or a mouse.

When at last you go home,
you'll recall the old Half Dome.
Formed in earth, so long past,
it rose up, to forever last. . .
in the forest, among the trees,
home to deer, bear, and bees.
(Bears need bees for the honey
they will eat when it is sunny.
So when it's sunny among trees,
remember there MAY be bears,
where there ARE bees!)

To see a world in a grain of sand,
And a heaven in a wild flower,
Hold infinity in the palm of your hand,
An eternity in an hour.

—William Blake—

www.ingramcontent.com/pod-product-compliance
Ingram Content Group UK Ltd.
Pitfield, Milton Keynes, MK11 3LW, UK
UKHW060136240426
12048UKWH00002B/66